A Lovely Sunday
for Creve Coeur

By TENNESSEE WILLIAMS

Tennessee Williams

A Lovely Sunday for Creve Coeur

A New Directions Book

CAUTION: Professionals and amateurs are hereby warned that *A Lovely Sunday for Creve Coeur*, being fully protected under the copyright laws of the United States of America, the British Commonwealth including the Dominion of Canada, and all other countries of the Copyright Union, is subject to royalty. All rights, including professional, amateur, motion picture, recitation, lecturing, public reading, radio and television broadcasting, and the rights of translation into foreign languages, are strictly reserved. Particular emphasis is laid on the question of readings, permission for which must be secured from the author's agent, The Lantz Office, 888 Seventh Avenue, New York 10106.

Inquiries concerning the amateur acting rights should be directed to The Dramatists' Play Service, Inc., 440 Park Avenue South, New York 10016, without whose permission in writing no amateur performance may be given.

Manufactured in the United States of America
New Directions Books are printed on acid-free paper.

First published clothbound and as New Directions
Paperbook 497 in 1980

Published simultaneously in Canada by
Penguin Books Canada Limited

Library of Congress Cataloging in Publication Data

Williams, Tennessee, 1911–1983
A Lovely Sunday for Creve Coeur.
(A New Directions Book)
I. Title.
PS3545.I5365L6   812'.5'4   79-20589
ISBN 0-8112-0756-0
ISBN 0-8112-0757-9 pbk.

New Directions Books are published for James Laughlin
by New Directions Publishing Corporation,
80 Eighth Avenue, New York 10011

FOURTH PRINTING

A Lovely Sunday for Creve Coeur

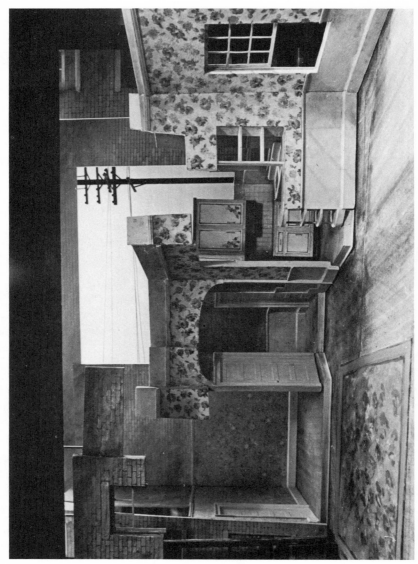

Photograph by Steven E. Moses

The New York premiere of *A Lovely Sunday for Creve Coeur* took place at the Hudson Guild Theatre on January 10, 1979. It was directed by Keith Hack; set design by John Conklin; lighting design by Craig Miller; costume design by Linda Fisher; producing director, Craig Anderson. The cast in order of appearance was as follows:

DOROTHEA	SHIRLEY KNIGHT
BODEY	PEG MURRAY
HELENA	CHARLOTTE MOORE
MISS GLUCK	JANE LOWRY

SCENE ONE

||||||||||||||||||||||||||||||||||||||||||||||||||||||||||||||||||||||||||||||||||||||||||||||||||||||||||||||||||||||

It is late on a Sunday morning, early June, in St. Louis.

The interior is what was called an efficiency apartment in the period of this play, the middle or late thirties. It is in the West End of St. Louis. Attempts to give the apartment brightness and cheer have gone brilliantly and disastrously wrong, and this wrongness is emphasized by the fiercely yellow glare of light through the oversize windows which look out upon vistas of surrounding apartment buildings, vistas that suggest the paintings of Ben Shahn: the dried-blood horror of lower middle-class American urban neighborhoods. The second thing which assails our senses is a combination of counting and panting from the bedroom, to the left, where a marginally youthful but attractive woman, Dorothea, is taking "setting-up exercises" with fearful effort.

SOUND: Ninety-one, *ha!* —ninety-two, *ha!* —ninety-three, *ha!* —ninety-four, *ha!*

This breathless counting continues till one hundred is achieved with a great gasp of deliverance. At some point during the counting, a rather short, plumpish woman, early middle-aged, has entered from the opposite doorway with a copy of the big Sunday *St. Louis Post-Dispatch.*

The phone rings just as Bodey, who is hard-of-hearing, sits down on a sofa in the middle of the room. Bodey, absorbed in the paper, ignores the ringing phone, but it has caused Dorothea to gasp with emotion so strong that she is physically frozen except for her voice. She catches hold of something for a moment, as if reeling in a storm, then plunges to the bedroom door and rushes out into the living room with a dramatic door-bang.

||||||||||||||||||||||||||||||||||||||||||||||||||||||||||||||||||||||||||||||||||||||||||||||||||||||||||||||||||||||

DOROTHEA: WHY DIDN'T YOU GET THAT PHONE?

1

BODEY [*rising and going to the kitchenette at the right*]: Where, where, what, what phone?

DOROTHEA: Is there more than one phone here? Are there several other phones I haven't discovered as yet?

BODEY: —Dotty, I think these setting-up exercises get you overexcited, emotional, I mean.

DOROTHEA [*continuing*]: That phone was ringing and I told you when I woke up that I was expecting a phone call from Ralph Ellis who told me he had something very important to tell me and would phone me today before noon.

BODEY: Sure, he had something to tell you but he didn't.

DOROTHEA: Bodey, you are not hearing, or comprehending, what I'm saying at all. Your face is a dead giveaway. I said Ralph Ellis—you've heard me speak of Ralph?

BODEY: Oh, yes, Ralph, you speak continuously of him, that name Ralph Ellis is one I got fixed in my head so I could never forget it.

DOROTHEA: Oh, you mean I'm not permitted to mention the name Ralph Ellis to you?

BODEY [*preparing fried chicken in the kitchenette*]: Dotty, when two girls are sharing a small apartment, naturally each of the girls should feel perfectly free to speak of whatever concerns her. I don't think it's possible for two girls sharing a small apartment *not* to speak of whatever concerns her whenever—whatever—*concerns* her, but, Dotty, I know that I'm not your older sister. However, if I was, I would have a suspicion that you have got a crush on this Ralph Ellis, and as an older sister, I'd feel obliged to advise you to, well, look before you

2

leap in that direction. I mean just don't put all your eggs in one basket till you are one hundred percent convinced that the basket is the right one, that's all I mean. . . . Well, this is a lovely Sunday for a picnic at Creve Coeur. . . . Didn't you notice out at Creve Coeur last Sunday how Buddy's slimmed down round the middle?

DOROTHEA: No, I didn't.

BODEY: Huh?

DOROTHEA: Notice.

BODEY: Well, it was noticeable, Dotty.

DOROTHEA: Bodey, why should I be interested in whatever fractional—fluctuations—occur in your twin brother's waist-line—as if it was the Wall Street market and I was a heavy investor?

BODEY: You mean you don't care if Buddy shapes up or not?

DOROTHEA: Shapes up for what?

BODEY: Nacherly for you, Dotty.

DOROTHEA: Does he regard me as an athletic event, the high jump or pole vault? Please, please, Bodey, convince him his shape does not concern me at all.

BODEY: Buddy don't discuss his work with me often, but lately he said his boss at Anheuser-Busch has got an eye on him.

DOROTHEA: How could his boss ignore such a sizeable object? —Bodey, what are you up to in that cute little kitchenette?

BODEY: Honey, I stopped by Piggly-Wiggly's yesterday noon

when I got off the streetcar on the way home from the office, and I picked up three beautiful fryers, you know, nice and plump fryers.

DOROTHEA: I'd better remain out here till Ralph calls back, so I can catch it myself. [*She lies on the purple carpet and begins another series of formalized exercises.*]

BODEY: The fryers are sizzling so loud I didn't catch that, Dotty. You know, now that the office lets out at noon Saturday, it's easier to lay in supplies for Sunday. I think that Roosevelt did something for the country when he got us half Saturdays off because it used to be that by the time I got off the street-car from International Shoe, Piggly-Wiggly's on the corner would be closed, but now it's still wide open. So I went in Piggly-Wiggly's, I went to the meat department and I said to the nice old man, Mr. Butts, the butcher, "Mr. Butts, have you got any real nice fryers?"—"You bet your life!" he said, "I must of been expectin' you to drop in. Feel these nice plump fryers." Mr. Butts always lets me feel his meat. The feel of a piece of meat is the way to test it, but there's very few modern butchers will allow you to feel it. It's the German in me. I got to feel the meat to know it's good. A piece of meat can look good over the counter but to know for sure I always want to feel it. Mr. Butts, being German, he understands that, always says to me, "Feel it, go on, feel it." So I felt the fryers. "Don't they feel good and fresh?" I said, "Yes, Mr. Butts, but will they keep till tomorrow?" "Haven't you got any ice in your ice-box?" he asked me. I said to him, "I hope so, but ice goes fast in hot weather. I told the girl that shares my apartment with me to put up the card for a twenty-five pound lump of ice but sometimes she forgets to." Well, thank goodness, this time you didn't forget to. You always got so much on your mind in the morning, civics and—other things at the high school. —What are you laughin' at, Dotty? [*She turns around to glance at Dorothea who is covering her mouth to stifle breathless sounds of laughter.*]

DOROTHEA: Honestly, Bodey, I think you missed your calling. You should be in Congress to deliver a filibuster. I never knew it was possible to talk at such length about ice and a butcher.

BODEY: Well, Dotty, you know we agreed when you moved in here with me that I would take care of the shopping. We've kept good books on expenses. Haven't we kept good books? We've never had any argument over expense or disagreements between us over what I should shop for. —OW!

DOROTHEA: Now what?

BODEY: The skillet spit at me. Some hot grease flew in my face. I'll put bakin' soda on it.

DOROTHEA: So you are really and truly frying chickens in this terrible heat?

BODEY: And boiling eggs, I'm going to make deviled eggs, too. Dotty, what is it? You sound hysterical, Dotty!

DOROTHEA [*half strangled with laughter*]: Which came first, fried chicken or deviled eggs? —I swear to goodness, you do the funniest things. Honestly, Bodey, you are a source of continual astonishment and amusement to me. Now, Bodey, please suspend this culinary frenzy until the phone rings again so you can hear it this time before it stops ringing for me.

BODEY: Dotty, I was right here and that phone was not ringin'. I give you my word that phone was not makin' a sound. It was quiet as a mouse.

DOROTHEA: Why, it was ringing its head off!

BODEY: Dotty, about some things everyone is mistaken, and this is something you are mistaken about. I think your exercises give you a ringing noise in your head. I think they're too

5

strenuous for you, 'specially on Sunday, a day of rest, recreation . . .

DOROTHEA: We are both entitled to separate opinions, Bodey, but I assure you I do not suffer from ringing in my head. That phone was RINGING. And why you did not hear it is simply because you don't have your hearing aid on!

[*The shouting is congruent with the fiercely bright colors of the interior.*]

BODEY: I honestly ain't that deaf. I swear I ain't that deaf, Dotty. The ear specialist says I just got this little calcification, this calcium in my—eardrums. But I do hear a telephone ring, a sharp, loud sound like that, I hear it, I hear it clearly.

DOROTHEA: Well, let's hope Ralph won't imagine I'm out and will call back in a while. But do put your hearing aid in. I don't share your confidence in your hearing a phone ring or a dynamite blast without it, and anyway, Bodey, you must adjust to it, you must get used to it, and after a while, when you're accustomed to it, you won't feel complete without it.

BODEY: —Yes, well— This is the best Sunday yet for a picnic at Creve Coeur . . .

DOROTHEA: That we'll talk about later. Jut put your hearing aid in before I continue with my exercises. Put it in right now so I can see you.

BODEY: You still ain't finished with those exercises?

DOROTHEA: I've done one hundred bends and I did my floor exercises. I just have these bust development exercises and my swivels and—BODEY! PUT YOUR HEARING AID IN!

6

BODEY: I hear you, honey, I will. I'll put it on right now.

[*She comes into the living room from the kitchenette and picks up the hearing aid and several large artificial flowers from a table. She hastily moves the newspaper from the sofa to a chair behind her, then inserts the device in an ear with an agonized look.*]

DOROTHEA: It can't be that difficult to insert it. Why, from your expression, you could be performing major surgery on yourself! . . . without anesthesia . . .

BODEY: I'm just—not used to it yet. [*She covers the defective ear with an artificial chrysanthemum.*]

DOROTHEA [*in the doorway*]: You keep reminding yourself of it by covering it up with those enormous artificial flowers. Now if you feel you have to do that, why don't you pick out a flower that's suitable to the season? Chrysanthemums are for autumn and this is June.

BODEY: Yes. June. How about this poppy?

DOROTHEA: Well, frankly, dear, that big poppy is tacky.

BODEY: —The tiger lily?

DOROTHEA [*despairing*]: Yes, the tiger lily! Of course, Bodey, the truth of the matter is that your idea of concealing your hearing aid with a big artificial flower is ever so slightly fantastic.

BODEY: —Everybody is sensitive about something . . .

DOROTHEA: But complexes, obsessions must not be cultivated. Well. Back to my exercises. Be sure not to miss the phone.

7

Ralph is going to call me any minute now. [*She starts to close the bedroom door.*]

BODEY: Dotty?

DOROTHEA: Yes?

BODEY: Dotty, I'm gonna ask Buddy to go to Creve Coeur with us again today for the picnic. That's okay with you, huh?

DOROTHEA [*pausing in the doorway*]: Bodey, Buddy is your brother and I fully understand your attachment to him. He's got many fine things about him. A really solid character and all that. But, Bodey, I think it's unfair to Buddy for you to go on attempting to bring us together because—well, everyone has a type she is attracted to and in the case of Buddy, no matter how much—I appreciate his sterling qualities and all, he simply isn't—[*She has gone into the bedroom and started swiveling her hips.*]

BODEY: Isn't what, Dotty?

DOROTHEA: A type that I can respond to. You know what I mean. In a romantic fashion, honey. And to me—romance is—essential.

BODEY: Oh—but—well, there's other things to consider besides—romance . . .

DOROTHEA [*swiveling her hips as she talks*]: Bodey, can you honestly feel that Buddy and I are exactly right for each other? Somehow I suspect that Buddy would do better looking about for a steady, German-type girl in South St. Louis—a girl to drink beer with and eat Wiener schnitzel and get fat along with him, not a girl—well, a girl already romantically—pour me a little more coffee? —Thanks. —Why do you keep forgetting the understanding between me and Mr. Ellis? Is that fair to Buddy? To build up his hopes for an inevitable letdown?

[*Dorothea stops her swivels and returns to the living room to get the coffee Bodey has poured for her.*]

BODEY: This Mr. T. Ralph Ellis, well . . .

DOROTHEA: Well, *what?*

BODEY: Nothing except . . .

DOROTHEA: *What?*

BODEY: He might not be as reliable as Buddy—in the long run.

DOROTHEA: What is "the long run," honey?

BODEY: The long run is—*life.*

DOROTHEA: Oh, so that is the long run, the long run is life! With Buddy? Well, then give me the short run, I'm sorry, but I'll take the short run, much less exhausting in the heat of the day and the night!

BODEY: Dotty, I tell you, Dotty, in the long run or the short run I'd place my bet on Buddy, not on a—fly-by-night sort of proposition like this, this—romantic idea you got about a man that mostly you see wrote up in—society pages . . .

DOROTHEA: *That is your misconception!* —Of something about which you are in total ignorance, because I rarely step out of the civics classroom at Blewett without seeing Ralph Ellis a few steps down the corridor, pretending to take a drink at the water cooler on my floor which is two floors up from his office!

BODEY: Not really taking a drink but just pretending? Not a good sign, Dotty—pretending . . .

DOROTHEA: What I mean is—we have to arrange secret little encounters of this sort to avoid gossip at Blewett.

BODEY: —Well—

DOROTHEA: *WHAT?*

BODEY: I never trusted pretending.

DOROTHEA: Then why the paper flowers over the hearing aid, dear?

BODEY: That's—just—a little—sensitivity, there . . .

DOROTHEA: Look, you've got to live with it so take off the concealment, the paper tiger lily, and turn the hearing aid up or I will be obliged to finish my hip swivels out here to catch Ralph's telephone call.

BODEY [*as she is turning up the hearing aid, it makes a shrill sound*]: See? See?

DOROTHEA: I think you mean hear, hear! —Turn it down just a bit, find the right level for it!

BODEY: Yes, yes, I—[*She fumbles with the hearing aid, dislodging the paper flower.*]

DOROTHEA: For heaven's sake, let me adjust it for you! [*She rushes over to Bodey and fiddles with the hearing aid.*] Now! —Not shrieking. —But can you hear me? I said can you hear me! At this level!?

10

BODEY: Yes. Where's my tiger lily?

DOROTHEA: Dropped on the fierce purple carpet. Here. [*She picks it up and hands it to Bodey.*] What's wrong with you?

BODEY: I'm—upset. Over this maybe—dangerous—trust you've got in Ralph Ellis's—intentions . . .

DOROTHEA [*dreamily, eyes going soft*]: I don't like discussing an intimate thing like this but—the last time I went out in Ralph Ellis's Reo, that new sedan he's got called the Flying Cloud . . .

BODEY: Cloud? Flying?

DOROTHEA [*raising her voice to a shout*]: The Reo is advertised as "The Flying Cloud."

BODEY: Oh. Yes. He'd be attracted to that.

DOROTHEA: It was pouring down rain and Art Hill was deserted, no other cars on it but Ralph and I in his Reo. The windows curtained with rain that glistened in the lamplight.

BODEY: Dotty, I hope you're not leading up to something that shouldn't of happened in this Flying Cloud on Art Hill. It really scares me, Dotty . . .

DOROTHEA: Frankly, I was a little frightened myself because— we've never had this kind of discussion before, it's rather—difficult for me but you must understand. I've always drawn a strict line with a man till this occasion.

BODEY: Dotty, do you mean—?

DOROTHEA: It was so magical to me, the windows curtained

11

with rain, the soft look in his eyes, the warmth of his breath
that's always scented with clove, his fingers touching so gently
as he—

BODEY: Dotty, I don't think I want to know any more about
this—experience on Art Hill because, because—I got a suspicion,
Dotty, that you didn't hold the line with him.

DOROTHEA: The line just—didn't exist when he parked the car
and turned and looked at me and I turned and looked at him.
Our eyes, our eyes—

BODEY: Your eyes?

DOROTHEA: Burned the line out of existence, like it had never
existed!

BODEY: —I'm not gonna tell this to Buddy!

DOROTHEA: You know, I wasn't aware until then that the Reo
was equipped with adjustable seats.

BODEY: Seats that—?

DOROTHEA: Adjusted to pressure, yes, reclined beneath me
when he pushed a lever.

BODEY [*distracted from the phonebook which she had begun
to leaf through*]: —How far did this seat recline beneath you,
Dotty?

DOROTHEA: Horizontally, nearly. So gradually though that I
didn't know till later, later. Later, not then—the earth was
whirling beneath me and the sky was spinning above.

BODEY: Oh-ho, he got you drunk, did he, with a flask of
liquor in that Flying Cloud on—

DOROTHEA: Drunk on a single Pink Lady?

BODEY: Pink?

DOROTHEA: Lady. —The mildest sort of cocktail! Made with sloe gin and grenadine.

BODEY: The gin was slow, maybe, but that man is a fast one, seducing a girl with adjustable seats and a flask of liquor in that Flying Cloud on—

DOROTHEA: Not a flask, a cocktail, and not in the Reo but in a small private club called The Onyx, a club so exclusive he had to present an engraved card at the entrance.

BODEY: Oh yes, I know such places!

DOROTHEA: How would you know such places?

BODEY: I seen one at the movies and so did you, at the West End Lyric, the last time you was all broke up from expectin' a call from this Ellis which never came in, so we seen Roy D'Arcy take poor Janet Gaynor to one of them—private clubs to—!

[*Bodey has not found the Blewett number in the phone-book. She dials the operator.*]

Blewett, Blewett, get me the high school named Blewett.

DOROTHEA: Bodey, what are you doing at the phone which I begged you not to use till Ralph has called?

BODEY: Reporting him to Blewett!

DOROTHEA: Bodey, that takes the cake, reporting on the principal of Blewett to Blewett that's closed on Sundays. What a remarkable—

13

BODEY [*darting about*]: Paper, pen!

DOROTHEA: Now what?

BODEY: A written report to the Board of Education of St. Louis. I tell you, that Board will be interested in all details of how that principal of the school system got you lying down drunk and defenseless in his Flying Cloud in a storm on Art Hill, every advantage taken with Valentino sheik tricks on a innocent teacher of civics just up from Memphis.

DOROTHEA: YOU WILL NOT—

BODEY: DON'T TELL ME NOT!

DOROTHEA: LIBEL THE REPUTATION OF A MAN THAT I LOVE, GAVE MYSELF TO NOT JUST FREELY BUT WITH ABANDON, WITH JOY!

BODEY [*aloud as she writes*]: Board of Education of St. Louis, Missouri. I think you should know that your principal at Blewett used his position to take disgusting advantage of a young teacher employed there by him for that purpose. I know, I got the facts, including the date and—

[*Dorothea snatches up and crumples the letter.*]

My letter, you tore up my—!

DOROTHEA: Bodey, if you had written and mailed that letter, do you know what you'd have obliged me to do? I would be morally obliged to go personally down to the Board of Education and tell them an *opposite* story which happens to be the *true* one: that I *desired* Ralph Ellis, possibly even more than he did me!

[*Bodey huffs and puffs wordlessly till she can speak.*]

14

BODEY: —Well, God help you, Dotty. —But I give you my word I won't repeat this to Buddy.

DOROTHEA: How does it concern Buddy?

BODEY: It concerns Buddy and me because Buddy's got deep feelings and respect for you, Dotty. He would respect you too much to cross the proper line before you had stood up together in the First Lutheran Church on South Grand.

DOROTHEA: *Now* you *admit* it!

BODEY: It's you that's makin' admissions of a terrible kind that might shock Buddy out of his serious intentions.

DOROTHEA: You are admitting that—

[*As she had threatened, Dorothea has begun doing her hip swivels in the living room, but now she stops and stares indignantly at Bodey.*]

—you've been deliberately planning and plotting to marry me off to your twin brother so that my life would be just one long Creve Coeur picnic, interspersed with knockwurst, sauer-kraut—hot potato salad dinners. —Would I be asked to prepare them? Even in summer? I know what you Germans regard as the limits, the boundaries of a woman's life—*Kirche, Küche, und Kinder*—while being asphyxiated gradually by cheap cigars. I'm sorry but the life I design for myself is not along those lines or in those limits. My life must include romance. Without romance in my life, I could no more live than I could without breath. I've got to find a partner in life, or my life will have no meaning. But what I must have and finally do have is an affair of the heart, two hearts, a true consummated romance —yes consummated, I'm not ashamed! [*She gasps and sways.*]

BODEY: Dotty, Dotty, set down and catch your breath!

15

DOROTHEA: In this breathless efficiency apartment? —I've got to have space in my life.

BODEY: —Did I tell you that Buddy has made a down payment on a Buick?

DOROTHEA: No, you didn't and why should you, as it does not concern— Oh, my God, Blessed Savior!

BODEY: Dotty, what Dotty? D'you want your, your whatamacallit tablets?

DOROTHEA: Mebaral? No, I have not collapsed yet, but you've just about driven me to it.

BODEY: Take a breather, take a seventh inning stretch while I—

DOROTHEA: Bodey, this room is GLARING; it's not cheerful but GLARING!

BODEY: Stretch out on the sofa and look up, the ceiling is white!

DOROTHEA: I don't know why I'm so out of breath today.

BODEY: Don't do no more exercises. You drink too much coffee an' Cokes. That's stimulants for a girl high-strung like you. With a nervous heart condition.

DOROTHEA: It's functional—not nervous.

BODEY: Lie down a minute.

DOROTHEA: I will rest a little—but not because you say so. [*Between gasps she sinks into a chair.*] You're very bossy— and very inquisitive, too.

16

BODEY: I'm older'n you, and I got your interests at heart.

DOROTHEA: Whew!

BODEY: Think how cool it will be on the open-air streetcar to Creve Coeur.

DOROTHEA: You must have had your hearing aid off when I said I had other plans.

BODEY: Buddy, I been telling Buddy to cut down on his beer, and Buddy is listening to me. He's cut down to eight a day—from a dozen and will cut down more . . .

DOROTHEA: Bodey, could you stop talking about Buddy this hot Sunday morning? It's not a suitable subject for hot weather. I know brother-sister relationships are deep, but it's not just the beer, it's the almost total lack of interests in common, no topics of conversations, of—of mutual—interest.

BODEY: They could develop. I know Buddy just feels embarrassed. He hasn't opened up yet. Give him time and he will.

DOROTHEA: Bodey, this discussion is embarrassingly pointless in view of the fact that I'm already committed to Ralph Ellis. I still have to do my hip swivels . . .

[*Sipping coffee as she goes, Dorothea returns to the bedroom and resumes her exercises.*]

BODEY [*rushing to the phone*]: Olive 2697, Olive 2697! Buddy? Me! *Grosser Gott!* I can't talk now, but you absolutley got to go to Creve Coeur with us this Sunday. —Dress good! Don't smoke cigars! And laugh at her witty remarks. —Well, they *are*, they're witty! She teaches *civics*.

17

[*The doorbell rings*].

Now be at the Creve Coeur station at 1:30, huh? —Please!—
Somebody's at the door, I can't talk now. [*Leaving the phone
off the hook, she rushes to the door and opens it.*] Oh. Hello.

HELENA: Good morning.

BODEY: Are you a friend of Dotty's?

[*A stylishly dressed woman with the eyes of a predatory
bird appears.*]

HELENA: Of Dorothea's? —Yes.

BODEY: Well, then come on in. Any friend of Dotty's is a
friend of mine.

HELENA: Is that so?

BODEY [*discomfited*]: Yes, I—got grease on my hand. I was
fryin' up some chickens for a picnic.

HELENA: —Well! This is a surprise! [*She makes several turns
in a mechanical, rigid fashion, eyes staring.*]

BODEY: Excuse me, I should of—interduced myself.

HELENA: You are Miss Bodenheifer.

BODEY: Hafer, not heifer. [*She laughs nervously.*] Heifer
meaning a cow.

HELENA: No conscious association whatsoever. [*She advances
forward a step.*] So this is Schlogger Haven?

18

BODEY: Oh, Schlogger Haven, that's just a joke of Dotty's. The landlord's name is Schlogger, that's all—that's all . . .

HELENA: Dorothea was joking, was she?

BODEY: Yeh, she jokes a lot, full of humor. We have lots of laughs. [*Bodey extends her hand.*]

HELENA: I can imagine you might, Miss Bodenheifer.

BODEY: You can forget the Miss. —Everyone at the office calls me Bodey.

HELENA: But we are not at the office—we are here in Schlogger Haven. [*She continues enigmatically.*] Hmmm . . . I've never ventured this side of Blewett before.

BODEY: Never gone downtown?

HELENA: I do nearly all my shopping in the West End, so naturally it amazed me to discover street after street without a shade tree on it, and the glare, the glare, and the heat refracted by all the brick, concrete, asphalt—was so overpowering that I nearly collapsed. I think I must be afflicted with a combination of photo- and heliophobia, both.

BODEY [*unconsciously retreating a step as if fearing contagion*]: I never heard of neither—but you got *both?*

HELENA: An exceptional sensitivity to both heat and strong light.

BODEY: Aw.

HELENA: Yes. Now would you please let Dorothea know I'm here to see her?

19

BODEY: Does Dotty expect you, Miss, uh—

HELENA: Helena Brookmire, no, she doesn't expect me, but a very urgent business matter has obliged me to drop by this early.

BODEY: She won't have no one in there with her. She's exercising.

HELENA: But Dorothea and I are well acquainted.

BODEY: Well acquainted or not acquainted at all, makes no difference. I think that modern girls emphasize too much these advertised treatments and keep their weight down too much for their health.

HELENA: The preservation of youth requires some sacrifices.

[*She continues to stare about her, blinking her birdlike eyes as if dazzled.*]

BODEY: —I guess you and Dotty teach together at Blewett High?

HELENA: —Separately.

BODEY: You mean you're not at Blewett where Dotty teaches civics?

HELENA [*as if addressing a backward child*]: I teach there, too. When I said separately, I meant we teach separate classes.

BODEY: Oh, naturally, yes. [*She tries to laugh.*] I been to high school.

HELENA: Have you?

20

BODEY: Yes. I know that two teachers don't teach in the same class at the same time, on two different subjects.

HELENA [*opening her eyes very wide*]: Wouldn't *that* be peculiar.

BODEY: Yes. That would be peculiar.

HELENA [*chuckling unpleasantly*]: It might create some confusion among the students.

BODEY: Yes, I reckon it would.

HELENA: Especially if the subjects were as different as civics and the history of *art*.

[*Bodey attempts to laugh again; Helena imitates the laugh almost exactly.*

[*Pause*]

This *is*, it really *is!*

BODEY: Is *what?*

HELENA: The most remarkable room that I've ever stepped into! Especially the combination of colors! Such a *vivid* contrast! May I sit down?

BODEY: Yeh, yeh, excuse me, I'm not myself today. It's the heat and the—

HELENA: Colors? —The vivid contrast of colors? [*She removes a pair of round, white-rimmed dark glasses from her purse and puts them on.*] Did Dorothea assist you, Miss Bodenheifer, in decorating this room?

BODEY: No, when Dotty moved in, it was just like it is now.

HELENA: Then you are solely responsible for this inspired selection of colors?

[*There is a loud sputter of hot fat from the kitchenette.*]

BODEY: Excuse me a moment, I got to turn over the fryers in the skillet.

HELENA: Don't let me interrupt your preparations for a picnic.

BODEY: Didn't catch that. I don't hear good sometimes.

HELENA: Oh?

BODEY: You see, I got this calcium deposit in my ears . . . and they advised me to have an operation, but it's very expensive for me and sometimes it don't work.

PHONE VOICE: Booow-deeee!

[*Helena notices but doesn't comment on the unhooked phone.*]

HELENA: I would advise you against it. I had an elderly acquaintance who had this calcification problem and she had a hole bored in her skull to correct it. The operation is called fenestration—it involves a good deal of danger and whether or not it was successful could not be determined since she never recovered consciousness.

BODEY: Never recovered?

HELENA: Consciousness.

BODEY: Yeh, well, I think maybe I'd better learn to live with it.

PHONE VOICE [*shouting again*]: Bodeyyyyy—Bodeyyyy—

BODEY: What's that?

HELENA: I was wondering, too. Very strange barking sounds are coming out of the phone.

BODEY [*laughing*]: Oh, God, I left it unhooked. [*She snatches it up.*] Buddy, sorry, somebody just dropped in, forgot you was still on the line. Buddy, call me back in a few minutes, huh, Buddy, it's, uh, very important. [*She hangs up the phone.*] That was my brother. Buddy. He says he drunk two beers and made him a liverwurst sandwich before I got back to the phone. Thank God he is so good-natured. . . . He and me are going out on a picnic at Creve Coeur with Dotty this afternoon. My brother is very interested in Dotty.

HELENA: Interested? Romantically?

BODEY: Oh, yes, Buddy's a very serious person.

HELENA [*rising*]: —I am very impressed!

BODEY: By what, what by?

HELENA [*with disguised fury*]: The ingenuity with which you've fitted yourself into this limited space. Every inch seems to be utilized by some appliance or—*decoration?* [*She picks up a large painted china frog.*] —A frahg?

BODEY: Yes, frawg.

HELENA: So realistically colored and designed you'd almost

23

expect it to croak. —Oh, and you have a canary . . . stuffed!

BODEY: Little Hilda . . . she lived ten years. That's the limit for a canary.

HELENA: Limit of longevity for the species?

BODEY: She broke it by three months.

HELENA: Establishing a record. It's quite heroic, enduring more than ten years in such confinement. What tenacity to existence some creatures do have!

BODEY: I got so attached to it, I took it to a, a—

HELENA: Taxidermist.

BODEY: Excuse me a moment. [*She rushes to the stove in the alcove.*] OW! —Got burnt again.

HELENA [*following curiously*]: You were burnt before?

[*Bodey profusely powders her arms with baking soda. Helena backs away.*]

Miss Bodenheifer, *please!* You've sprinkled my clothes with that powder!

BODEY: Sorry, I didn't mean to.

HELENA: Intentional or not, I'm afraid you have! May I have a clothes brush?

BODEY: Look at that, I spilt it on the carpet. [*She rushes to fetch a broom.*]

HELENA: Miss Bodenheifer, I WOULD LIKE A CLOTHES BRUSH, IF YOU HAVE A *CLOTHES* BRUSH! Not a broom. I am not a carpet.

BODEY: AW. SURE. Dotty's got a clothes brush. Oh. Help yourself to some coffee. [*She drops the broom and enters the bedroom.*]

[*Through the open door, Dorothea can be heard counting as she swivels.*]

DOROTHEA'S VOICE: Sixty, *ha!* Sixty-one, *ha!* [*She continues counting but stops when she notices Bodey.*] —The PHONE? Is it the PHONE?

BODEY: Clothes brush. [*Bodey closes the bedroom door and begins opening and shutting drawers as she looks for the clothes brush.*]

DOROTHEA: DON'T, DON'T, DON'T—slam a drawer shut like that! I feel like screaming!

[*Helena opens a closet in the kitchenette; a box falls out.*]

HELENA: The hazards of this place almost equal the horrors.

DOROTHEA [*in the bedroom*]: I asked you if the phone rang.

BODEY: No, no, the doorbell.

HELENA [*who has moved to the icebox*]: Ah. Ice, mostly melted, what squalor!

[*This dual scene must be carefully timed.*]

DOROTHEA: I presume it's Miss Gluck from upstairs in boudoir

25

cap and wrapper. Bodey, get her out as quickly as possible. The sight of that woman destroys me for the whole day.

HELENA [*still in the kitchenette*]: This remnant of ice will not survive in this steaming glass of coffee.

[*A knock at the door is heard.*]

What's that?

[*Sophie Gluck opens the front door and sticks her head in. At the sight of Helena, she withdraws in alarm.*]

Another tenant. *Demented!*

[*Helena moves to the door and slams and bolts it with such force that Sophie, outside, utters a soft cry of confused panic.*]

BODEY: Don't do no more calisthenics if it affecks you this way.

DOROTHEA: Just, just—knock at the door when Miss Gluck has gone back upstairs, that's my—whew!—only—request . . .

BODEY: —Yes, well . . .

DOROTHEA: No coffee, no crullers or she—will stay—down here—forever—ha!

[*The phone rings; Helena picks it up. Bodey emerges from the bedroom with a whisk broom, closing the door behind her. Helena is at the phone.*]

HELENA: Oh, she seems engaged for the moment . . .

BODEY: Aw, the phone! Is it that principal, Ellis?

HELENA [*aside from the phone*]: I'm afraid not. It seems to be Dorothea's other admirer—*quel embarras de richesses* . . .

BODEY [*rushing to the phone*]: Must be Buddy. —Buddy? Well? —Yeh, good, what suit you got on? Well, take it off. It don't look good on you, Buddy. Put on the striped suit, Buddy an' the polka dot tie, and, Buddy, if you smoke a cigar at Creve Coeur, excuse yourself and smoke it in the bushes.

HELENA: This is—

BODEY: That's right, 'bye.

HELENA: —absolutely bizarre! You found a clothes brush? That's not a clothes brush. It's a whisk broom. Sorry. It doesn't look clean.

BODEY: Sorry. My nerves.

HELENA [*taking it and brushing herself delicately here and there*]: What was that counting I heard? Is Dorothea counting something in there?

BODEY: She's counting her swivels in there.

HELENA: Swivels of what?

BODEY: Hip swivels, that's what. She's counting. Every morning she does one hundred bends and one hundred set-ups and one hundred hip swivels.

HELENA: Regardless of weather?

BODEY: That's right, regardless of weather.

HELENA: And regardless of— Hmmm . . .

[*Bodey senses a touch of malice implicit in this unfinished
sentence.*]

BODEY: —What else, huh?

HELENA: Dorothea has always impressed me as an emotionally
fragile type of person who might collapse, just suddenly collapse, when confronted with the disappointing facts of a situation about which she'd allowed herself to have—romantic illu-
sions.

[*It is now Bodey's turn to say, "Hmmm . . ."*]

—No matter how—well, I hate to say foolish but even intelli-
gent girls can make mistakes of this nature . . . of course we
all felt she was attaching too much importance to—

BODEY: "We all" is who?

HELENA: Our little group at Blewett.

BODEY: Yeh, there's always a gossipy little group, even down
at International Shoe where I work there is a gossipy little
group that feels superior to the rest of us. Well, personally, I
don't want in with this gossipy little group because the gossip is
malicious. Oh, they call it being concerned, but it's not the
right kind of concern, naw, I'd hate for that gossipy little group
to feel concerned about me, don't want that and don't need it.

HELENA: Understandably, yaiss. I will return this whisk broom
to Dorothea.

BODEY: No, no, just return it to me.

HELENA: I have to speak to her and in order to do that I'll
have to enter that room. So if you'll excuse me I'll—

[*She starts toward the bedroom. Bodey snatches the whisk broom from her with a force that makes Helena gasp.*]

BODEY: Miss Brooksit, you're a visitor here but the visit was not expected. Now you excuse me but I got to say you sort of act like this apartment was yours.

HELENA: —What a dismaying idea! I mean I—

BODEY: And excuse me or don't excuse me but I got a very strong feeling that you got something in mind. All right, your mind is your mind, what's in it is yours but keep it to yourself, huh?

HELENA [*cutting in*]: Miss Bodenheifer, you seem to be implying something that's a mystery to me.

BODEY: You know what I mean and I know what I mean so where's the mystery, huh?

DOROTHEA [*calling from the bedroom*]: Is somebody out there, Bodey?

BODEY: Just Sophie Gluck.

DOROTHEA: Oh, Lord!

HELENA: What was that you called me?

BODEY: I told Dotty that you was Miss Gluck from upstairs.

HELENA: —Gluck?

BODEY: Yeah, Miss Gluck is a lady upstairs that comes downstairs to visit.

HELENA: She comes down to see Dorothea?

BODEY: No, no, more to see me, and to drink coffee. She lost her mother, an' she's got a depression so bad she can't make coffee, so I save her a cup, keep her a cup in the pot. You know for a single girl to lose a mother is a terrible thing. What else can you do? She oughta be down. Weekdays she comes down at seven. Well, this is Sunday.

HELENA: Yes. This is Sunday.

BODEY: Sundays she comes down for coffee and a cruller at ten.

HELENA: Cruller? What is a cruller?

BODEY: Aw. You call it a doughnut, but me, bein' German, was raised to call it a cruller.

HELENA: Oh. A cruller is a doughnut but you call it a cruller. Now if you'll excuse me a moment, I will go in there and relieve Dorothea of the mistaken impression that I am Miss Gluck from upstairs who has come down for her coffee and—cruller.

BODEY: Oh, no, don't interrupt her calisthenics.

[*Helena ignores this admonition and opens the bedroom door.*]

DOROTHEA: Why, Helena Brookmire! —What a surprise. I— I—look a—*mess!*

HELENA: I heard this counting and gasping. Inquired what was going on. Your friend Miss—what?

DOROTHEA: You've met Miss Bodenhafer?

30

HELENA: Yes, she received me very cordially. We've dispensed with introductions. She says any friend of yours is a friend of hers and wants me to call her Bodey as they do at the office. Excuse me, Miss Bodenheifer, I must have a bit of private conversation—

[*Helena closes the bedroom door, shutting out Bodey.*]

DOROTHEA: Well, I wasn't expecting a visitor today, obviously not this early. You see, I—never receive a visitor here. . . . Is there something too urgent to hold off till Monday, Helena?

HELENA: Have our negotiations with the realty firm of Orthwein and Muller slipped your flighty mind?

DOROTHEA: Oh, the real estate people, but surely on Sunday—

HELENA: Mr. Orthwein called Cousin Dee-Dee last night and she called me this morning that now the news has leaked out and there's competitive bidding for the apartment on Westmoreland Place and the deal must be settled at once.

DOROTHEA: You mean by—?

HELENA: Immediate payment, yes, to pin it down.

DOROTHEA: *Today? Sunday?*

HELENA: The sanctity of a Sunday must sometimes be profaned by business transactions.

[*Bodey has now entered.*]

DOROTHEA: Helena, if you'll just have some coffee and wait in the living room, I will come out as soon as I've showered and dressed.

31

BODEY: Yeh, yeh, do that. You're embarrassing Dotty, so come back out and—

[*Bodey almost drags Helena out of the bedroom, kicking the bedroom door shut.*]

HELENA: Gracious!

BODEY: Yes, gracious, here! Set down, I'll get you some coffee.

HELENA [*with a sharp laugh*]: She said, "I look a mess," and I couldn't contradict her.

BODEY: Here! Your coffee! Your cruller!

HELENA [*haughtily*]: I don't care for the cruller, as you call it. Pastries are not included in my diet. However—I'd like a clean napkin. You've splashed coffee everywhere.

BODEY: Sure, we got plenty of napkins. You name it, we got it. [*She thrusts a paper napkin at Helena like a challenge.*]

HELENA: This paper napkin is stained. Would you please give me—

BODEY: Take 'em all. You stained that napkin yourself. [*She thrusts the entire pile of napkins at Helena.*]

HELENA: You shoved the cup at me so roughly the coffee splashed.

[*Helena fastidiously wipes the tabletop. There is a rap at the door.*]

BODEY: Aw, that's Sophie Gluck.

32

HELENA: I don't care to meet Miss Gluck.

BODEY: Will you set down so I can let in Sophie Gluck?

HELENA: So if you're going to admit her, I will take refuge again in Dorothea's bedroom. . . . There is another matter I've come here to . . .

BODEY [*seizing Helena's arm as she crosses toward the bedroom*]: I know what you're up to! —JUST A MINUTE, *BITTE,* SOPHIE! I can guess the other matter you just can't hold your tongue about, but you're gonna hold it. It's not gonna be mentioned to cloud over the day and spoil the Creve Coeur picnic for Dotty, Buddy, an' me! —COMIN', SOPHIE! [*Then, to Helena, fiercely.*] YOU SET BACK DOWN!

[*During this altercation, Dorothea has been standing in the bedroom paralyzed with embarrassment and dismay. Now she calls sweetly through the door, opened a crack.*]

DOROTHEA: Bodey, Bodey, what *is* going on out there? How could a phone be heard above that shouting? Oh, My Blessed Savior, I was bawn on a Sunday, and I am convinced that I shall die on a Sunday! Could you please tell me what is the cause of the nerve-shattering altercations going on out there?

HELENA: Dorothea, Miss Bodenheifer's about to receive Miss Gluck.

DOROTHEA: Oh, no, oh no, Bodey, entertain her upstairs! I'm not in shape for another visit today, especially not—Bodey!

BODEY: Sophie, Sophie, you had me worried about you.

HELENA: I'm afraid, Dorothea, your request has fallen upon a calcified eardrum.

33

BODEY: You come downstairs so late.

MISS GLUCK: *Sie hat die Tür in mein Kopf zugeschlagen!*

BODEY [*to Helena*]: You done that to Sophie!

HELENA: An unknown creature of demented appearance entering like a sneak thief!

BODEY: My best friend in the building!

HELENA: What a pitiful admission!

BODEY: You come here uninvited, not by Dotty or me, since I never heard of you, but got the nerve to call my best friend in the building . . .

MISS GLUCK: *Diese Frau ist ein Spion.*

BODEY: What did you call her?

HELENA: I called that woman demented. What I would call you is intolerably offensive.

MISS GLUCK: *Verstehen Sie?* Spy. *Vom Irrenhaus.*

BODEY: We live here, you don't. See the difference?

HELENA: Thank God for the difference. *Vive la différence.*

DOROTHEA [*coming just inside the living room*]: Helena, Bodey.

HELENA: Be calm Dorothea—don't get overexcited.

MISS GLUCK: *Zwei Jahre.* Two years.

DOROTHEA: Why is she coming at me like this?

MISS GLUCK: State asylum.

BODEY: You come here to scrounge money outta Dotty which she ain't got.

MISS GLUCK: *Sie ist hier—mich noch einmal—im Irrenhaus zu bringen.* To take back to hospital.

HELENA: Aside from the total inaccuracy of your assumption and the insulting manner in which you express it—. As you very well know, Dorothea and I are both employed at Blewett. We are both on salary there! And I have not come here to involve myself in your social group but to rescue my colleague from it.

BODEY: Awright, you put it your way, it adds up to the same thing. You want money from Dotty which she ain't got to give you. Dotty is broke, flat broke, and she's been on a big buying spree, so big that just last night I had to loan her the price of a medium bottle of Golden Glow Shampoo, and not only that, I had to go purchase it for her because she come home exhausted. Dotty was too exhausted to walk to the drugstore. Well, me, I was tired, too, after my work at International Shoe and shopping, but out I hoofed it to Liggett's and forked out the forty-nine cents for the medium size Golden Glow from my own pockets, money I set aside for incidentals at the Creve Coeur picnic. There's always—

HELENA [*cutting in*]: Miss Bodenheifer, you certainly have a gift for the felicitous phrase such as "out you hoofed it to Liggett's," sorry, sorry, but it does evoke an image.

BODEY: I know what you mean by "hoof it" since you keep repeating "heifer" for "hafer." I'm not too dumb like which

35

you regard me to know why you're struck so funny by "hoof it."

HELENA: You said you "hoofed it," not me.

BODEY: You keep saying "heifer" for "hafer." Me, I'm a sensitive person with feelings I feel, but sensitive to you I am not. Insults from you bounce off me. I just want you to know that you come here shaking your tin cup at the wrong door.

[*As a soft but vibrant counterpoint to this exchange, Sophie, sobbing and rolling her eyes like a* religieuse *in a state of sorrowful vision, continues her slow shuffle toward Dorothea as she repeats in German an account of her violent ejection by Helena.*]

DOROTHEA [*breathlessly*]: Bodey, what is she saying? Translate and explain to her I have no knowledge of German.

HELENA: Babbling, just lunatic babbling!

BODEY: One minute, one minute, Dotty. I got to explain to this woman she's wasting her time here and yours—and had the moxie to slam Sophie out of the door.

HELENA: Miss Bodenheifer, it's useless to attempt to intimidate me. . . . I would like the use of your phone for a moment. Then—

DOROTHEA: No calls on the phone!

BODEY: Dotty don't want this phone used; she's expecting a call to come in, but there is a pay phone at Liggett's three blocks east on West Pine and Pearl.

HELENA: Drugstores are shut on Sundays!

DOROTHEA: Quiet! Listen! All! This thing's getting out of hand!

HELENA: I want only to call a taxi for myself and for Dorothea. She's trapped here and should be removed at once. You may not know that just two weeks after she came to Blewett she collapsed on the staircase, and the staff doctor examined her and discovered that Dorothea's afflicted with neuro-circulatory asthenia.

[*Dorothea has disappeared behind the sofa. Miss Gluck is looking down at her with lamentations.*]

MISS GLUCK: BODEY.

BODEY: Moment, Sophie.

MISS GLUCK: Dotty, Dotty . . .

HELENA: What is she saying? Where's Dorothea?

BODEY: Dotty?

MISS GLUCK: *Hier, auf dem Fussboden. Ist fallen.*

HELENA: This Gluck creature has thrown Dorothea onto the floor.

BODEY: *Gott im*—! *Wo ist*—Dotty?

HELENA: The Gluck has flung her to the floor behind the sofa!

BODEY: Dotty!

HELENA: Dorothea, I'm calling us a cab. Is she conscious?

37

DOROTHEA: Mebaral—tablet—quick!

BODEY: Mebarals, where?

[*Sophie wails loudly.*]

DOROTHEA: My pocketbook!

BODEY: Hold on now, slowly, slowly—

DOROTHEA: Mebaral! Tablets!

HELENA: My physician told me those tablets are only pre-
scribed for persons with—extreme nervous tension and asthenia.

BODEY: Will you goddam shut up? —Dotty, you just need
to—

HELENA: What she needs is to stop these strenuous exercises
and avoid all future confrontations with that lunatic from
upstairs!

BODEY: Dotty, let me lift you.

DOROTHEA: Oh, oh, noooo, I—can't, I—I am *paralyzed, Bodey!*

BODEY: HEY, YOU BROOKS-IT, TAKE DOTTY'S
OTHER ARM. HELP ME CARRY HER TO HER BED
WILL YUH?

[*Sophie is moaning through clenched fists.*]

HELENA: All right, all right, but then I shall call my physician!

[*Dorothea is carried into the bedroom and deposited on the
bed. Sophie props pillows behind her.*]

DOROTHEA: Meb—my meb . . .

BODEY: Tablets. Bathroom. In your pocketbook.

[*Bodey rushes into the bathroom, then out with a small bottle. Dorothea raises a hand weakly and Bodey drops tablets in it.*]

Dotty, don't swallow, that's three tablets!

DOROTHEA: My sherry to wash it down with—

BODEY: Dotty, take out the *two extra tablets,* Dotty!

HELENA: Sherry? Did she say sherry? Where is it?

DOROTHEA: There, there.

BODEY: Dotty, open your mouth, I got to take out those extras!

HELENA: No glass, you must drink from the bottle.

BODEY: NO! NOOOO!

HELENA: STOP CLUTCHING AT ME!

[*Miss Gluck utters a terrified wail. Dorothea drinks from the bottle and falls back onto the pillows with a gasp.*]

BODEY [*so angry she speaks half in German*]: You *Schwein,* you bitch! *Alte böse Katze.* [*She then goes on in English.*] You washed three tablets down Dotty!

DOROTHEA: Now will you BOTH get out so I can breathe!

HELENA: The door's obstructed by Gluck.

39

BODEY: Sophie, go out, Sophie, go out of here with me for coffee and crullers!

[*Sobbing, Sophie retreats. Bodey grabs a strong hold of Helena's wrist.*]

HELENA: Let go of my wrist. Oh, my God, you have broken. . . . I heard a bone snap in my—!

BODEY: WALK! OUT! MOVE IT! . . .

HELENA [*turning quickly about and retreating behind the sofa*]: Miss Bodenheifer, you are a one-woman demonstration of the aptness of the term "Huns" for Germans. . . . And, incidentally, what you broke was not my wrist but my Cartier wristwatch, a birthday present from my Cousin Dee-Dee; you shattered the crystal, and you've broken the minute hand and bent the two others. I am afraid the repair bill will cost you considerably more than keeping Dorothea in Golden Glow Shampoo.

BODEY: It's all right, Sophie, set down right here and I'll. . . . Coffee's still hot for you. Have a coupla crullers. Blow your nose on this napkin and—

[*Helena laughs tonelessly.*]

What's funny, is something funny? You never been depressed, no sorrows in your life ever, yeh, and you call yourself a human.

HELENA: Really, this is fantastic as the—color scheme of this room or the—view through the windows.

[*In the bedroom, Dorothea has staggered from the bed and stumbled to the floor.*]

DOROTHEA: Bodey.

HELENA: Dorothea.

BODEY [*calling through*]: Dotty.

HELENA: You really must let me check on her condition.

DOROTHEA [*in the bedroom*]: Don't forget . . . phone call.

BODEY: No, Dotty.

DOROTHEA [*faintly, clinging to something*]: Tell Miss Brookmire I've retired for the day.

HELENA: *What?*

BODEY: She's not coming out. She's not coming out till you leave here—

[*Bodey bolts the bedroom door.*]

HELENA: I beg to differ. She *will* and I'll sit here till she does!

[*Miss Gluck has taken a bite of a cruller, dunked in coffee, and begins to blubber, the coffee-soaked cruller dribbling down her chin.*]

BODEY: Look, you upset Sophie!

MISS GLUCK: *Eine—Woche vor—Sonntag—meine Mutter—*

BODEY [*comfortingly*]: *Ich weiss*, Sophie, *ich weiss.*

MISS GLUCK: *Gestorben!*

BODEY: But she went *sudden*, huh, Sophie? [*She crouches be-*

41

side Miss Gluck, removing the dribblings of cruller and coffee from her mouth and chin.]

HELENA: I don't understand the language, and the scene appears to be private.

BODEY: Yeh, keep out of it. [*She turns to Miss Gluck.*]— Your mother, she didn't hang on like the doctor thought she would, Sophie. Now, face it, it was better sudden, no big hospital bill, just went and is waiting for you in Heaven.

HELENA: With open arms, I presume, and with coffee and crullers.

BODEY: So, Sophie, just be grateful that she went quick with no pain.

MISS GLUCK [*grotesquely tragic*]: *Nein, nein, sie hat geschrien!* I woke up runnin'!

BODEY: To her bed, you reached it and she was dead. Just one scream, it was over—wasn't that a mercy?

[*Helena laughs.*]

Sophie, honey, this woman here's not sympathetic. She laughs at sorrow, so maybe you better take the coffee, the cruller— here's another—upstairs, Sophie, and when we get back from the Creve Coeur picnic, I will bring you beautiful flowers, *schöne Blume.* Then I'll come up and sing to you in German— I will sing you to sleep.

[*Miss Gluck slowly rises with coffee and crullers. Bodey conducts her gently to the door.*]

MISS GLUCK [*crying out*]: *Ich bin allein, allein! In der Welt, freundlos!*

BODEY: No, no, Sophie, that is negative thinking.

MISS GLUCK: *Ich habe niemand in der Welt!*

BODEY: Sophie, God is with you, I'm with you. Your mother, all your relations are waiting for you in Heaven!

[*Shepherding Miss Gluck into the hall, Bodey repeats this assurance in German.*]

HELENA: Sometimes despair is just being realistic, the only logical thing for certain persons to *feel*. [*She addresses herself with a certain seriousness, now.*] Loss. Despair. I've faced them and actually they have—fortified and protected, not overcome me at all . . .

BODEY [*in the hall with Miss Gluck*]: Okay? *Verstehst du,* Sophie?

HELENA [*still ruminating privately*]: The weak. The strong. Only important division between living creatures. [*She nods birdlike affirmation.*]

[*Miss Gluck remains visible in the hall, afraid to return upstairs.*]

MISS GLUCK: *Allein, allein.*

[*There is a change in the light. Helena moves a small chair downstage and delivers the following to herself.*]

HELENA: *Allein, allein* means alone, alone. [*A frightened look appears in her eyes.*] Last week I dined alone, alone three nights in a row. There's nothing lonelier than a woman dining alone, and although I loathe preparing food for myself, I cannot bear the humiliation of occupying a restaurant table for one. Dining *au solitaire!* But I would rather starve than reduce my social

43

standards by accepting dinner invitations from that middle-aged gaggle of preposterously vulgar old maids that wants to suck me into their group despite my total ,abhorrence of all they stand for. Loneliness in the company of five intellectually destitute spinsters is simply loneliness multiplied by five . . .

[*There is a crash in the hallway.*]

DOROTHEA [*from the bedroom*]: Is it the phone?

HELENA: Another visit so soon? Miss Bodenheifer, your bereaved friend from upstairs is favoring you with another visit.

MISS GLUCK [*wildly*]: *Mein Zimmer is gespukt, gespukt!*

HELENA: "Spooked, spooked"?

BODEY: Sophie, your apartment isn't haunted.

HELENA: Perhaps if you went up with her, it would despook the apartment.

BODEY: Aw, no, I got to stay down and keep a sharp eye on *you.*

HELENA: Which means that she will remain here?

BODEY: Long as she pleases to. What's it to you? She got nothin' contagious. You can't catch heartbreak if you have got no heart.

HELENA: May I suggest that you put her in the back yard in the sun. I think that woman's complexion could stand a touch of color.

BODEY: I am puttin' her nowhere she don't want to be. How

44

about you settin' in the back yard? Some natural color would do your face good for a change.

[*Sensing the hostile "vibes," Miss Gluck moans, swaying a little.*]

HELENA: Miss Bodenheifer, I will not dignify your insults with response or attention!

[*Miss Gluck moans louder.*]

Aren't you able to see that this Miss Gluck is mental? Distressing to hear and to look at! . . . Be that as it may, I shall wait.

BODEY: Sitting? Tight as a tombstone? Huh?

HELENA: I can assure you that for me to remain in this place is at least as unpleasant to me as to you. [*She cries out to Dorothea who is still in the bedroom.*] Dorothea? Dorothea? Can you hear me?

DOROTHEA [*clinging to something in the bedroom*]: See you— Blewett—t'morrow . . .

HELENA: No, no, at once, Dorothea, the situation out here is dreadful beyond endurance.

[*Abruptly, Miss Gluck cries out, clutching her abdomen.*]

BODEY: Sophie, what is it, Sophie?

MISS GLUCK: *Heisser Kaffee gibt mir immer Krampf und Durchfall.*

[*This episode in the play must be handled carefully to avoid excessive scatology but keep the humor.*]

45

BODEY: You got the runs? *Zum Badezimmer?* Sophie's got to go to the bathroom, Dotty.

DOROTHEA: Hasn't she got one upstairs?

BODEY: After hot coffee, it gives her diarrhea!

DOROTHEA: Must she have it down here?

MISS GLUCK [*in German*]: *KANN NICHT WARTEN!*

BODEY: She can't wait, here, bathroom, Sophie! *Badezimmer!*

[*Miss Gluck rushes through the bedroom into the bathroom.*]

DOROTHEA: What a scene for Helena to report at Blewett. Miss Gluck, turn on both water faucets full force.

BODEY: Sophie, *beide Wasser rennen.*

DOROTHEA: Bodey, while I am here don't serve her hot coffee again since it results in these—crises!

BODEY: Dotty, you know that Sophie's got this problem.

DOROTHEA: Then send her coffee upstairs.

BODEY: Dotty, you know she needs companionship, Dotty.

DOROTHEA: That I cannot provide her with just now!

[*Bodey returns to the living room.*]

HELENA: How did Dorothea react to Miss Gluck's sudden indisposition?

46

BODEY: Dotty's a girl that understands human afflictions.

[*There is a crash in the bathroom.*]

DOROTHEA: Phone, Ralph's call—has he—did he?

BODEY: Phone, Dotty? No, no phone.

HELENA: I wouldn't expect—

BODEY [*to Helena*]: Watch it!

HELENA: Watch what, Miss Bodenheifer? What is it you want me to watch?

BODEY: That mouth of yours, the tongue in it, with such a tongue in a mouth you could dig your grave with like a shovel!

HELENA [*her laughter tinkling like ice in a glass*]: —The syntax of that sentence was rather confusing. You know, I suspect that English is not your native language but one that you've not quite adequately adopted.

BODEY: I was born on South Grand, a block from Tower Grove Park in this city of St. Louis!

HELENA: Ah, the German section. Your parents were German speaking?

BODEY: I learned plenty English at school, had eight grades of school and a year of business college.

HELENA: I see, I see, forgive me. [*She turns to a window, possibly in the "fourth wall."*] Is a visitor permitted to look out the window?

47

BODEY: A visitor like you's permitted to jump out it.

HELENA [*laughing indulgently*]: With so many restrictions placed on one's speech and actions—

[*Bodey turns up her hearing aid so high that it screeches shrilly.*]

DOROTHEA: Is it the phone?

HELENA: Please. Is it controllable, that electric hearing device?

BODEY: What did you say?

[*The screeching continues.*]

HELENA: Ow . . . ow . . .

[*Bodey finally manages to turn down the hearing aid.*]

DOROTHEA: Oh please bring a mop, Bodey. Water's streaming under—the bathroom door. Miss Gluck's flooded the bathroom.

BODEY: What? Bring?

HELENA: *Mop, mop!*

[*Helena moves toward the bedroom door but Bodey shoves her back.*]

BODEY: Stay! Put! Stay put!

[*Bodey grabs a mop from the closet and then rushes into the bedroom.*]

DOROTHEA: See? Water? Flooding?

BODEY: You told her to turn on both faucets. SOPHIE! *Halte das Wasser ab,* Sophie! [*Bodey opens the bathroom door and thrusts in the mop.*] Here, *das Wust, das Wust,* Sophie!

DOROTHEA [*to herself*]: This is incredible to me, I simply do not believe it! [*She then speaks to Bodey who has started back toward the living room.*] May I detain you a moment? The truth has finally struck me. Ralph's calls have been intercepted. He has been repeatedly calling me on that phone, and you have been just as repeatedly lying to me that he hasn't.

BODEY: LYING TO—?

DOROTHEA: YES, LYING! [*She stumbles to the door of the bedroom.*] Helena, will *you* please watch that phone for me now?

HELENA [*crossing to the bedroom door*]: I'm afraid, Dorothea, that a watched phone never rings!

[*Bodey emerges from the bedroom. She and Helena return to the living room while Dorothea retreats to the bed, shutting the door behind her.*]

What a view through this window, totally devoid of—why, no, a living creature, a pigeon! Capable of flight but perched for a moment in this absolute desolation . . .

INTERVAL

SCENE TWO

The scene is the same as before. The spotlight focuses on the lefthand, "bedroom" portion of the stage where Dorothea, seated at her vanity table and mellowed by her mebaral and sherry "cocktail," soliloquizes.

DOROTHEA [*taking a large swallow of sherry*]: Best years of my youth thrown away, wasted on poor Hathaway James. [*She removes his picture from the vanity table and with closed eyes thrusts it out of sight.*] Shouldn't say wasted but so unwisely devoted. Not even sure it was love. Unconsummated love, is it really love? More likely just a reverence for his talent—precocious achievements . . . musical prodigy. Scholarship to Juilliard, performed a concerto with the Nashville Symphony at fifteen. [*She sips more sherry.*] But those dreadful embarrassing evenings on Aunt Belle's front porch in Memphis! He'd say: "Turn out the light, it's attracting insects." I'd switch it out. He'd grab me so tight it would take my breath away, and invariably I'd feel plunging, plunging against me that—that—frantic part of him . . . then he'd release me at once and collapse on the porch swing, breathing hoarsely. With the corner gas lamp shining through the wisteria vines, it was impossible not to notice the wet stain spreading on his light flannel trousers. . . . Miss Gluck, MOP IN!!

[*Miss Gluck, who has timidly opened the bathroom door and begun to emerge, with the mop, into the bedroom, hastily retreats from sight.*]

Such afflictions—visited on the gifted. . . . Finally worked up the courage to discuss the—Hathaway's—problem with the family doctor, delicately but clearly as I could. "Honey, this Hathaway fellow's afflicted with something clinically known as—chronic case of—premature ejaculation—must have a large

51

laundry bill. . . ." "Is it curable, Doctor?" —"Maybe with great patience, honey, but remember you're only young once, don't gamble on it, relinquish him to his interest in music, let him go."

[*Miss Gluck's mop protrudes from the bathroom again.*]

MISS GLUCK, I SAID MOP IN. REMAIN IN BATH-ROOM WITH WET MOP TILL MOP UP COMPLETED. MERCIFUL HEAVENS.

[*Helena and Bodey are now seen in the living room.*]

HELENA: Is Dorothea attempting a conversation with Miss Gluck in there?

BODEY: No, no just to herself—you gave her the sherry on top of mebaral tablets.

HELENA: She talks to herself? That isn't a practice that I would encourage her in.

BODEY: She don't need no encouragement in it, and as for you, I got an idea you'd encourage nobody in nothing.

DOROTHEA [*in the bedroom*]: After Hathaway James, there was nothing left for me but—CIVICS.

HELENA [*who has moved to the bedroom door the better to hear Dorothea's "confessions"*]: This is not to B. B.!

BODEY: Stop listening at the door. Go back to your pigeon watching.

HELENA: How long is this apt to continue?

52

DOROTHEA: Oh, God, thank you that Ralph Ellis has no such affliction—is healthily aggressive.

HELENA: I have a luncheon engagement in La Due at two!

BODEY: Well, go keep it! On time!

HELENA: My business with Dorothea must take precedence over anything else! [*Helena pauses to watch with amused suspicion as Bodey "attacks" the Sunday* Post-Dispatch *which she has picked up from the chair.*] What is that you're doing, Miss Bodenheifer?

BODEY: Tearing a certain item out of the paper.

HELENA: A ludicrous thing to do since the news will be all over Blewett High School tomorrow.

BODEY: Never mind tomorrow. There's ways and ways to break a piece of news like that to a girl with a heart like Dotty. You wouldn't know about that, no, you'd do it right now—malicious! —You got eyes like a bird and I don't mean a songbird.

HELENA: Oh, is that *so?*

BODEY: Yeh, yeh, that's so, I know!

[*Pause. Bodey, who has torn out about half of the top page of one section, puts the rest of the paper on the sofa, and takes the section from which the piece has been torn with her as she crosses to the kitchenette, crumpling and throwing the torn piece into the wastebasket on her way.*]

HELENA: Miss Bodenheifer.

BODEY [*from the kitchenette*]: Hafer!

HELENA: I have no wish to offend you, but surely you're able to see that for Dorothea to stay in these circumstances must be extremely embarrassing to her at least.

BODEY: Aw, you think Dotty's embarrassed here, do you?

[*Bodey has begun to line a shoebox with the section of newspaper she took with her. During the following exchange with Helena, Bodey packs the fried chicken and other picnic fare in the shoebox.*]

HELENA: She has hinted it's almost intolerable to her. The visitations of this Gluck person who has rushed to the bathroom, this nightmare of clashing colors, the purple carpet, orange drapes at the windows looking out at that view of brick and concrete and asphalt, lamp shades with violent yellow daisies on them, and wallpaper with roses exploding like bombshells, why it would give her a breakdown! It's giving me claustrophobia briefly as I have been here. Why, this is not a place for a civilized person to possibly exist in!

BODEY: What's so civilized about you, Miss Brooks-it? Stylish, yes, civilized, no, unless a hawk or a buzzard is a civilized creature. Now you see, you got a tongue in your mouth, but I got one in mine, too.

HELENA: You are being hysterical and offensive!

BODEY: You ain't heard nothing compared to what you'll hear if you continue to try to offer all this concern you feel about Dotty to Dotty in this apartment.

HELENA: Dorothea Gallaway and I keep nothing from each other and naturally I intend, as soon as she has recovered, to

54

prepare her for what she can hardly avoid facing sooner or later and I—

BODEY [*cutting in*]: I don't want heartbreak for Dotty. For Dotty I want a—life.

HELENA: A life of—?

BODEY: A life, a *life*—

HELENA: You mean as opposed to a death?

BODEY: Don't get smart with me. I got your number the moment you come in that door like a well-dressed snake.

HELENA: So far you have compared me to a snake and a bird. Please decide which—since the archaeopteryx, the only known combination of bird and snake, is long extinct!

BODEY: Yes, well, you talk with a kind of a hiss. Awright, you just hiss away but not in this room which you think ain't a civilized room. Okay, it's too cheerful for you but for me and Dotty it's fine. And this afternoon, at the picnic at Creve Coeur Lake, I will tell Dotty, gentle, in my own way, if it's necessary to tell her, that this unprincipled man has just been using her. But Buddy, my brother Buddy, if in some ways he don't suit her like he is now, I will see he quits beer, I will see he cuts out his cigars, I will see he continues to take off five pounds a week. And by Dotty and Buddy there will be children—children! —I will never have none, myself, no! But Dotty and Buddy will have beautiful kiddies. Me? Nieces—nephews. . . . —Now you! I've wrapped up the picnic. It's nice and cool at Creve Coeur Lake and the ride on the open-air streetcar is lickety-split through green country and there's flowers you can pull off the bushes you pass. It's a fine excursion. Dotty will forget not gettin' that phone call. We'll stay out till it's close to dark and the fireflies—fly. I will slip away and Buddy will be alone with her on the lake shore. He will smoke no smelly cigar. He will just respectfully hold her hand and say—"I love you, Dotty. Please be mine," not meanin' a girl in a car parked up on Art Hill but—for the long run of life.

HELENA: —Can Dorothea be really attached to your brother? Is it a mutual attraction?

BODEY: Dotty will settle for Buddy. She's got a few reservations about him so far, but at Creve Coeur she'll suddenly recognize the—wonderful side of his nature.

HELENA: Miss Bodenheifer, Dorothea is not intending to remain in this tasteless apartment. Hasn't she informed you that she is planning to share a lovely apartment with me? The upstairs of a duplex on Westmoreland Place?

BODEY: Stylish? Civilized, huh? And too expensive for you to swing it alone, so you want to rope Dotty in, rope her into a place that far from Blewett? Share expenses? You prob'ly mean pay most.

HELENA: To move from such an unsuitable environment must naturally involve some expense.

[*Miss Gluck falls out of the bathroom onto Dorothea's bed.*]

DOROTHEA: MISS GLUCK! CAREFUL! Bodey, Bodey, Sophie Gluck's collapsed on my bed in a cloud of steam!

HELENA: Has Miss Gluck broken a steam pipe?

[*Bodey rushes from the kitchenette into the bedroom.*]

BODEY [*to Helena*]: You stay out.

56

[*Dorothea emerges from the bedroom. She closes the door and leans against it briefly, closing her eyes as if dizzy or faint.*]

HELENA: At last.

DOROTHEA: I'm so mortified.

HELENA: Are you feeling better?

DOROTHEA: Sundays are always different—

HELENA: This one exceptionally so.

DOROTHEA: I don't know why but—I don't quite understand why I am so—agitated. Something happened last week, just a few evenings ago that—

HELENA: Yes? What?

DOROTHEA: Nothing that I'm—something I can't discuss with you. I was and still am expecting a very important phone call—

HELENA: May I ask you from whom?

DOROTHEA: No, please.

HELENA: Then may I hazard a guess that the expected call not received was from a young gentleman who cuts a quite spectacular figure in the country club set but somehow became involved in the educational system?

DOROTHEA: If you don't mind, Helena, I'd much prefer not to discuss anything of a—private nature right now.

HELENA: Yes, I understand, dear. And since you've located that chair, why don't you seat yourself in it?

57

DOROTHEA: Oh, yes, excuse me. [*She sits down, weakly, her hand lifted to her throat.*] The happenings here today are still a bit confused in my head. I was doing my exercises before you dropped by.

HELENA: And for quite a while after.

DOROTHEA: I was about to—no, I'd taken my shower. I was about to get dressed.

HELENA: But the Gluck intervened. Such discipline! Well! I've had the privilege of an extended meeting with Miss Bodenheifer—[*She lowers her voice.*] She seemed completely surprised when I mentioned that you were moving to Westmoreland Place.

DOROTHEA: Oh, you told her. —I'm glad. —I'm such a coward, I couldn't.

HELENA: Well, I broke the news to her.

DOROTHEA: I—just hadn't the heart to.

[*Miss Gluck advances from the bedroom with a dripping wet mop and a dazed look.*]

HELENA [*to Dorothea*]: Can't you see she's already found a replacement?

DOROTHEA: Oh, no, there's a limit even to Bodey's endurance! Miss Gluck, would you please return that wet mop to the kitchen and wring it out. *Küche*—mop—Sophie.

HELENA: Appears to be catatonic.

DOROTHEA [*as she goes into the bedroom to get Bodey*]: Excuse me.

[*Bodey enters from the bedroom and takes Miss Gluck, with mop, into the kitchenette.*]

BODEY [*singing nervously in the kitchenette*]: "I'm just breezing along with the breeze, pleasing to live, and living to please!"

[*Dorothea returns to the living room.*]

DOROTHEA: How did Bodey take the news I was moving?

HELENA: "That far from *Blewett!*" she said as if it were transcontinental.

DOROTHEA: Well, it is a bit far, compared to this location.

HELENA: Surely you wouldn't compare it to *this* location.

DOROTHEA: Oh, no, Westmoreland Place is a—fashionable address, incomparable in that respect, but it is quite a distance. Of course, just a block from Delmar Boulevard and the Olive Street car-line, that would let me off at—what point closest to Blewett?

HELENA: Dorothea, forget transportation, that problem. We're going by automobile.

DOROTHEA: By—what automobile do you—?

HELENA: I have a lovely surprise for you, dear.

DOROTHEA: Someone is going to drive us?

HELENA: Yes, I will be the chauffeur and you the passenger, dear. You see, my wealthy cousin Dee-Dee, who lives in La Due, has replaced her foreign-made car, an Hispano-Suiza, no less, practically brand-new, with a Pierce Arrow limousine and has offered to sell us the Hispano for just a song! Immediately, as soon as she made me this offer, I applied for a driver's license.

[*A moment of shocked silence is interrupted by a short squawk from Bodey's hearing aid.*]

BODEY [*advancing quickly from the kitchenette*]: Limazine? What limazine? With a show-fer?

HELENA: Miss Bodenheifer, how does this concern you?

BODEY: Who's gonna foot the bill for it, that's how!

HELENA: My cousin Dee-Dee in La Due will accept payment on time.

BODEY: Whose time and how much?

HELENA: *Negligible! A rich cousin!* —Oh, my Lord, I've always heard that Germans—

BODEY: Lay off Germans!

HELENA: Have this excessive concern with money matters.

BODEY: *Whose* money?

HELENA: Practicality can be a stupefying—

MISS GLUCK: Bodey?

HELENA: —virtue, if it *is* one.

MISS GLUCK: *Ich kann nicht*—go up.

60

HELENA: Go up just one step to the kitchen! Please, Dorothea, can't we—have a private discussion, briefly?

MISS GLUCK: *Das Schlafzimmer* is *gespukt!*

HELENA: Because you see, Dorothea, as I told you, I do have to make a payment on the Westmoreland Place apartment early tomorrow, and so must collect your half of it today.

DOROTHEA: —My half would amount to—?

HELENA: Seventy.

DOROTHEA: Ohhh! —Would the real estate people accept a—postdated check?

HELENA: Reluctantly—very.

DOROTHEA: You see, I had unusually heavy expenses this week—clothes, lingerie, a suitcase . . .

HELENA: Sounds as if you'd been purchasing a trousseau. —Miss Bodenhafer says that her brother, "Buddy," is seriously interested in you. How selfish of you to keep it such a secret!—even from me!

DOROTHEA: Oh, my heavens, has Miss Bodenhafer—how fantastic!

HELENA: Yes, she is a bit, to put it politely.

DOROTHEA: I meant has she given you the preposterous impression that I am interested in her brother? Oh, my Lord, what a fantàstic visit you've had! Believe me, the circumstances aren't always so—chaotic. Well! *Il n'y a rien à faire.* When I tell you that she calls her brother Buddy and that he is her *twin!* [*She throws up her arms.*]

61

HELENA: Identical?

DOROTHEA: Except for gender, alike as two peas in a pod. You're not so gullible, Helena, that you could really imagine for a moment that I'd—you know me better than that!

HELENA: Sometimes when a girl is on the rebound from a disappointing infatuation, she will leap without looking into the most improbable sort of—liaison—

DOROTHEA: Maybe some girls, but certainly not I. And what makes you think that I'm the victim of a "disappointing infatuation," Helena?

HELENA: Sometimes a thing will seem like the end of the world, and yet the world continues.

DOROTHEA: I personally feel that my world is just beginning. . . . Excuse me for a moment. I'll get my checkbook. . . .

[*Dorothea goes into the bedroom. Miss Gluck wanders back into the living room from the kitchenette, wringing her hands and sobbing.*]

HELENA: MISS BODENHEIFER!

BODEY: Don't bother to tell me good-bye.

HELENA: I am not yet leaving.

BODEY: And it ain't necessary to shake the walls when you call me, I got my hearing aid on.

HELENA: Would you be so kind as to confine Miss Gluck to that charming little kitchen while I'm completing my business with Dorothea?

[*Bodey crosses toward Miss Gluck.*]

BODEY: Sophie, come in here with me. You like a deviled egg don't you? And a nice fried drumstick when your— digestion is better? Just stay in here with me.

[*Bodey leads Miss Gluck back to the kitchenette, then turns to Helena.*]

I can catch every word that you say to Dotty in there, and you better be careful the conversation don't take the wrong turn!

MISS GLUCK [*half in German*]: *Ich kann nicht* liven opstairs no more, *nimmer, nimmer—kann nicht*—can't go!

BODEY: You know what, Sophie? You better change apart-ments. There's a brand-new vacancy. See—right over there, the fifth floor. It's bright and cheerful—I used to go up there sometimes—it's a sublet, furnished, everything in cheerful colors. I'll speak to Mr. Schlogger, no, no, to *Mrs.* Schlogger, she makes better terms. Him, bein' paralyzed, he's got to accept 'em, y'know.

MISS GLUCK: I think— [*She sobs.*] —Missus Schlogger don't like me.

BODEY: That's—*impossible*, Sophie. I think she just had a little misunderstanding with your—[*She stops herself.*]

MISS GLUCK: *Meine Mutter, ja—*

BODEY: Sophie, speak of the Schloggers, she's wheeling that old *Halunke* out on their fire escape.

[*The Schloggers are heard from offstage.*]

MR. SCHLOGGER'S VOICE: I didn't say *out* in the sun.

MRS. SCHLOGGER'S VOICE: You said out, so you're out.

BODEY [*shouting out the window*]: Oh, my *Gott*, Missus Schlogger, a stranger that didn't know you would think you meant to push him offa the landin'. Haul him back in, you better. Watch his cane, he's about to hit you with it. Amazin' the strength he's still got in his good arm.

MRS. SCHLOGGER'S VOICE: Now you want back in?

[*Helena rises to watch this episode on the fire escape.*]

MR. SCHLOGGER'S VOICE: Not in the kitchen with you.

HELENA [*to herself but rather loudly*]. Schloggers, so those are Schloggers.

BODEY [*to Miss Gluck*]: She's got him back in. I'm gonna speak to her right now. —HEY MISSUS SCHLOGGER, YOU KNOW MISS GLUCK? AW, SURE YOU REMEMBER SOPHIE UPSTAIRS IN 4–F? SHE LOST HER MOTHER LAST SUNDAY. Sophie, come here, stick your head out, Sophie. NOW YOU REMEMBER HER, DON'T YOU?

MRS. SCHLOGGER'S VOICE: *Ja, ja.*

BODEY: *JA, JA,* SURE YOU REMEMBER! MRS. SCHLOGGER, POOR SOPHIE CAN'T LIVE ALONE IN 4–F WHERE SHE LOST HER MOTHER. SHE NEEDS A NEW APARTMENT THAT'S BRIGHT AND CHEERFUL TO GET HER OUT OF DEPRESSION. HOW ABOUT THE VACANCY ON THE FIFTH FLOOR FOR

SOPHIE. WE GOT TO LOOK OUT FOR EACH OTHER
IN TIMES OF SORROW. *VERSTEHEN SIE?*

MRS. SCHLOGGER'S VOICE: I don't know.

BODEY: GIVE SOPHIE THAT VACANCY UP THERE.
THEN TERMS I'LL DISCUSS WITH YOU. [*She draws
Miss Gluck back from the window.*] Sophie, I think that done
it, and that apartment on five is bright and cheerful like here.
And you're not gonna be lonely. We got three chairs at this
table, and we can work out an arrangement so you can eat
here with us, more economical that way. It's no good cooking
for one, cookin' and eatin' alone is—lonely after—

[*Helena resumes her seat as Bodey and Miss Gluck return
to the kitchenette.*]

HELENA [*with obscure meaning*]: Yes— [*She draws a long
breath and calls out.*] Dorothea, can't you locate your checkbook in there?

[*Dorothea returns from the bedroom wearing a girlish
summer print dress and looking quite pretty.*]

DOROTHEA: I was just slipping into a dress. Now, then, here
it is, my checkbook.

HELENA: Good. Where did you buy that new dress?

DOROTHEA: Why, at Scruggs-Vandervoort.

HELENA: Let me remove the price tag. [*As she removes the
tag, she looks at it and assumes an amused and slightly superior
air.*] Oh, my dear. I must teach you where to find the best
values in clothes. In La Due there is a little French boutique,
not expensive but excellent taste. I think a woman looks best

65

when she dresses without the illusion she's still a girl in her teens. Don't you?

DOROTHEA [*stung*]: —My half will be—how much did you say?

HELENA: To be exact, $82.50.

DOROTHEA: My goodness, that will take a good bite out of my savings. Helena, I thought you mentioned a lower amount. Didn't you say it would be seventy?

HELENA: Yes, I'd forgotten—utilities, dear. Now, we don't want to move into a place with the phone turned off, the lights off. Utilities must be *on*, wouldn't you say?

DOROTHEA: —Yes. —Of course, I don't think I'll be dependent on my savings much longer, and a duplex on Westmoreland Place— [*She writes out a check.*] —is a—quite a—worthwhile —investment . . .

HELENA: I should think it would strike you as one after confinement with Miss Bodenhafer in this nightmare of colors.

DOROTHEA: Oh. —Yes. —Excuse me . . . [*She extends the check slightly.*]

HELENA: —Are you holding it out for the ink to dry on it?

DOROTHEA: —Sorry. —Here. [*She crosses to Helena and hands the check to her.*]

[*Helena puts on her glasses to examine the check carefully. She then folds it, puts it into her purse, and snaps the purse shut.*]

HELENA: Well, that's that. I hate financial dealings but they do have to be dealt with. Don't they?

DOROTHEA: Yes, they seem to . . .

HELENA: Require it. —Oh, contract.

DOROTHEA: Contract? For the apartment?

HELENA: Oh, no, a book on contract bridge, the bidding system and so forth. You do play bridge a little? I asked you once before and you said you did sometimes.

DOROTHEA: Here?

HELENA: Naturally not here. But on Westmoreland Place I hope you'll join in the twice-weekly games. You remember Joan Goode?

DOROTHEA: Yes, vaguely. Why?

HELENA: We were partners in duplicate bridge, which we usually played, worked out our own set of bidding conventions. But now Joan's gone to Wellesley for her Master's degree in, of all things, the pre-Ptolemaic dynasties of Egypt.

DOROTHEA: Did she do that? I didn't know what she did.

HELENA: You were only very casually—

DOROTHEA: Acquainted.

HELENA: My cousin Dee-Dee from La Due takes part whenever her social calendar permits her to. She often sends over dainty little sandwiches, watercress, tomato, sherbets from Zeller's in the summer. And a nicely uniformed maid to serve.

Well, now we're converting from auction to contract, which is more complicated but stimulates the mind. —Dorothea, you have an abstracted look. Are you troubled over something?

DOROTHEA: Are these parties mixed?

HELENA: "Mixed" in what manner?

DOROTHEA: I mean would I invite Ralph?

HELENA: I have a feeling that Mr. T. Ralph Ellis might not be able to spare the time this summer. And anyway, professional women do need social occasions without the—male intrusion . . .

DOROTHEA [*with spirit*]: I've never thought of the presence of men as being an intrusion.

HELENA: Dorothea, that's just a lingering symptom of your Southern belle complex.

DOROTHEA: In order to be completely honest with you, Helena, I think I ought to tell you—I probably won't be able to share expenses with you in Westmoreland Place for very long, Helena!

HELENA: Oh, is that so? Is that why you've given me the postdated check which you could cancel tomorrow?

DOROTHEA: You know I wouldn't do that, but—

HELENA: Yes, but—you could and possibly you would. . . . Look before you, there stands the specter that confronts you . . .

DOROTHEA: Miss??

HELENA: Gluck, the perennial, the irremediable, Miss Gluck! You probably think me superficial to value as much as I do, cousin Dee-Dee of La Due, contract bridge, possession of an elegant foreign car. Dorothea, only such things can protect us from a future of descent into the Gluck abyss of surrender to the bottom level of squalor. Look at it and tell me honestly that you can afford not to provide yourself with the Westmoreland Place apartment . . . its elevation, its style, its kind of *éclat.*

[*Miss Gluck, who has come out of the kitchenette and moved downstage during Helena's speech, throws a glass of water in Helena's face.*]

DOROTHEA: Bodey, RESTRAIN HER, RESTRAIN MISS GLUCK, SHE'S TURNED VIOLENT.

BODEY: Sophie, no, no. I didn't say you done wrong. I think you done right. I don't think you did enough.

HELENA: Violence does exist in the vegetable kingdom, you see! It doesn't terrify me since I shall soon be safely out of its range. . . . Just let me draw two good deep breaths and I'll be myself again. [*She does so.*] That did it. . . . I'm back in my skin. Oh, Dorothea, we must, must advance in appearances. You don't seem to know how vastly important it is, the move to Westmoreland Place, particularly now at this time when you must escape from reminders of, specters of, that alternative there! Surrender without conditions . . .

DOROTHEA: Sorry. I am a little abstracted. Helena, you sound as if you haven't even suspected that Ralph and I have been dating . . .

HELENA: Seriously?

69

DOROTHEA: Well, now that I've mentioned it to you, yes, quite. You see, I don't intend to devote the rest of my life to teaching civics at Blewett. I dream, I've always dreamed, of a marriage someday, and I think you should know that it might become a reality this summer.

HELENA: With whom?

DOROTHEA: Why, naturally with the person whom I love. And obviously loves me.

HELENA: T? RALPH? ELLIS?

[*Bodey, still in the kitchenette, nervously sings "Me and My Shadow."*]

DOROTHEA: I thought I'd made that clear, thought I'd made everything clear.

HELENA: Oh, Dorothea, my dear. I hope and pray that you haven't allowed him to take advantage of your—generous nature.

DOROTHEA: Miss Bodenhafer has the same apprehension.

HELENA: That is the one and only respect in which your friend, Miss Bodenhafer, and I have something in common.

DOROTHEA: Poor Miss Bodenhafer is terribly naïve for a girl approaching forty.

HELENA: Miss Bodenhafer is not approaching forty. She has encountered forty and continued past it, undaunted.

DOROTHEA: I don't believe she's the sort of girl who would conceal her age.

70

HELENA [*laughing like a cawing crow*]: Dorothea, no girl could tell me she's under forty and still be singing a song of that vintage. Why, she knows every word of it, including— what do they call it? The introductory verse? Why is she cracking hard-boiled eggs in there?

DOROTHEA: She's making deviled eggs for a picnic lunch.

HELENA: Oh. In Forest Park.

DOROTHEA: No, at Creve Coeur.

HELENA: Oh, at Creve Coeur, that amusement park on a lake, of which Miss Bodenheifer gave such a lyrical account. Would you like a Lucky?

DOROTHEA: No. Thank you. My father smoked Chesterfields. Do you know Creve Coeur?

HELENA: Heard of it. Only. You go out, just the two of you?

DOROTHEA: No, her brother, Buddy, usually goes with us on these excursions. They say they've been going out there since they were children, Bodey and Buddy. They still ride the Ferris wheel, you know, and there's a sort of loop-the-loop that takes you down to the lake shore. Seats much too narrow sometimes. You see, it's become embarrassing to me lately, the brother you know . . .

HELENA: Who doesn't interest you?

DOROTHEA: Heavens, no, it's—pathetic. I don't want to hurt Bodey's feelings, but the infatuation is hardly a mutual thing and it never could be, of course, since I am—well, involved with—

71

HELENA: The dashing, the irresistible new principal at Blewett.

[*Bodey sings.*]

DOROTHEA: —I'd rather not talk about that—prematurely, you know. Ralph feels it's not quite proper for a principal to be involved with a teacher. He's—a very, very scrupulous young man.

HELENA: Oh? Is that the impression he gives you? I'm rather surprised he's given you that impression.

DOROTHEA: I don't see why. Is it just because he's young and attractive with breeding, background? Frequently mentioned in the social columns? Therefore beyond involvement with a person of my ignominious position.

HELENA: Personally, I'd avoid him like a—snakebite!

[*Bodey, in the kitchenette, sings "I'm Just Breezing along with the Breeze" again.*]

Another one of her oldies! The prospect of this picnic at Creve Coeur seems to make her absolutely euphoric.

DOROTHEA: I'm afraid that they're the high points in her life. Sad . . . Helena, I'm very puzzled by your attitude toward Ralph Ellis. Why on earth would a girl want to avoid a charming young man like Ralph?

HELENA: Perhaps you'll understand a little later.

[*Dorothea glances at her watch and the silent phone.*]

DOROTHEA [*raising her voice*]: Bodey, please not quite so loud in there! Miss Brookmire and I are holding a conversation in here, you know. [*She turns back to Helena and continues the conversation with an abrupt vehemence.*] —Helena, that woman wants to absorb my life like a blotter, and I'm not an ink splash! I'm sorry you had to meet her. I'm awfully—embarrassed, believe me.

HELENA: I don't regret it at all. I found her most amusing. Even the Gluck!

DOROTHEA [*resuming with the same intensity*]: Bodey wants me to follow the same, same old routine that she follows day in and day out and I—feel sympathy for the loneliness of the girl, but we have nothing, nothing, but *nothing* at all, in common. [*She interrupts herself.*] Shall we have some coffee?

HELENA: Yes, please. I do love iced coffee, but perhaps the ice is depleted.

BODEY [*from the kitchenette*]: She knows darn well she used the last piece.

HELENA: Is it still warm?

[*Dorothea has risen and gone into the kitchenette where she pours two cups of coffee.*]

DOROTHEA: It never cools off in this electric percolator, runs out, but never cools off. Do you take cream?

HELENA: No, thank you.

DOROTHEA [*bringing the coffee into the living room*]: Bodey does make very good coffee. I think she was born and raised in a kitchen and will probably die in a kitchen if ever she does break her routine that way.

[*Bodey crosses to the kitchen table with Dorothea's purse*

*and hat which she has collected from the living room while
Helena and Dorothea sip their coffee.*]

BODEY: Dotty, remember, Buddy is waiting for us at the
Creve Coeur station, we mustn't let him think we've stood
him up.

DOROTHEA [*sighing*]: Excuse me, Helena, there really has
been a terrible problem with communication today. [*She
crosses to Bodey and adjusts her hearing aid for her.*] Can you
hear me clearly, now at last?

BODEY: You got something to tell me?

DOROTHEA: Something I've told you already, frequently,
loudly, and clearly, but which you simply will not admit because of your hostility toward Ralph Ellis. I'm waiting here to
receive an important call from him, and I am not going any-
where till it's come through.

BODEY: Dotty. It's past noon and he still hasn't called.

DOROTHEA: On Saturday evenings he's out late at social affairs
and consequently sleeps late on Sundays.

BODEY: This late?

HELENA: Miss Bodenhafer doesn't know how the privileged
classes live.

BODEY: No, I guess not, we're ignorant of the history of art,
but Buddy and me, we've got a life going on, you understand,
we got a life . . .

DOROTHEA: Bodey, you know I'm sorry to disappoint your
plans for the Creve Coeur picnic, but you must realize by now

—after our conversation before Miss Brookmire dropped in— that I can't allow this well-meant design of yours to get me involved with your brother to go any further. So that even if I were *not* expecting this important phone call, I would not go to Creve Coeur with you and your brother this afternoon—or ever! It wouldn't be fair to your brother to, to—lead him on that way . . .

BODEY: Well, I did fry up three chickens and I boiled a dozen eggs, but, well, that's—

HELENA: Life for you, Miss Bodenhafer. We've got to face it.

BODEY: But I really was hoping—expecting—

[*Tears appear in Bodey's large, childlike eyes.*]

HELENA: Dorothea, I believe she's beginning to weep over this. Say something comforting to her.

DOROTHEA: Bodey? Bodey? This afternoon you must break the news to your brother that—much as I appreciate his attentions—I am seriously involved with someone else, and I think you can do this without hurting his feelings. Let him have some beer first and a—cigar. . . . And about this superabundance of chicken and deviled eggs, Bodey, why don't you call some girl who works in your office and get her to go to Creve Coeur and enjoy the picnic with you this afternoon?

BODEY: Buddy and I, we—don't have fun with—strangers . . .

DOROTHEA: Now, how can you call them strangers when you've been working in the same office with these girls at International Shoe for—how many years? Almost twenty? Strangers? Still?

BODEY: —Not all of 'em have been there long as me . . . [*She blows her nose.*]

DOROTHEA: Oh, some of them must have, surely, unless the death rate in the office is higher than—a cat's back.

[*Dorothea smiles half-apologetically at Helena. Helena stifles a malicious chuckle.*]

BODEY: —You see, Dotty, Buddy and me feel so at home with you now.

DOROTHEA: Bodey, we knew that I was here just for a while because it's so close to Blewett. Please don't make me feel *guilty*. I have no reason to, do I?

BODEY: —No, no, Dotty—but don't worry about it. Buddy and me, we are both—big eaters, and if there's somethin' left over, there's always cute little children around Creve Coeur that we could share with, Dotty, so—

DOROTHEA: Yes, there must be. Do that. Let's not prolong this discussion. I see it's painful to you.

BODEY: —Do you? No. It's—you I'm thinking of, Dotty. —Now if for some reason you should change your mind, here is the schedule of the open-air streetcars to Creve Coeur.

HELENA: Yellowing with antiquity. Is it legible still?

BODEY: We'll still be hoping that you might decide to join us, you know that, Dotty.

DOROTHEA: Yes, of course—I know that. Now why don't you finish packing and start out to the station?

BODEY: —Yes. —But remember how welcome you would be if—shoes. [*She starts into the bedroom to put on her shoes.*] I still have my slippers on.

DOROTHEA [*to Helena after Bodey has gone into the bedroom*]: So! You've got the postdated check. I will move to Westmoreland Place with you July first, although I'll have to stretch quite a bit to make ends meet in such an expensive apartment.

HELENA: Think of the advantages. A fashionable address, two bedrooms, a baby grand in the front room and—

DOROTHEA: Yes, I know. It would be a very good place to entertain Ralph.

HELENA: I trust that entertaining Ralph is not your only motive in making this move to Westmoreland Place.

DOROTHEA: Not the only, but the principal one.

HELENA [*leaning forward slowly, eyes widening*]: Oh, my dear Dorothea! I have the very odd feeling that I saw the name Ralph Ellis in the newspaper. In the society section.

DOROTHEA: In the society section?

HELENA: I think so, yes. I'm sure so.

[*Rising tensely, Dorothea locates the Sunday paper which Bodey had left on the sofa, in some disarray, after removing the "certain item"—the society page. She hurriedly looks through the various sections trying to find the society news.*]

DOROTHEA: Bodey? —BOOO-DEYY!

BODEY: What, Dotty?

DOROTHEA: Where is the society page of the *Post-Dispatch?*

BODEY: —Oh . . .

DOROTHEA: What does "oh" mean? It's disappeared from the paper and I'd like to know where.

BODEY: Dotty, I—

DOROTHEA: What's wrong with you? Why are you upset? I just want to know if you've seen the society page of the Sunday paper?

BODEY: —Why, I—used it to wrap fried chicken up with, honey.

DOROTHEA [*to Helena*]: The only part of the paper in which I have any interest. She takes it and wraps fried chicken in it before I get up in the morning! You see what I mean? Do you understand now? [*She turns back to Bodey.*] Please remove the fried chicken from the society page and *let me have it!*

BODEY: —Honey, the chicken makes the paper so greasy that—

DOROTHEA: *I will unwrap it myself!* [*She charges into the kitchenette, unwraps the chicken, and folds out the section of pages.*] —A section has been torn out of it? Why? What for?

BODEY: Is it? I—

DOROTHEA: Nobody possibly could have done it but you. What did you do with the torn out piece of the paper?

78

BODEY: —I— [*She shakes her head helplessly.*]

DOROTHEA: Here it is! —Crumpled and tossed in the waste-basket!—What for, I wonder? [*She snatches up the crumpled paper from the wastebasket and straightens it, using both palms to press it hard against the kitchen table so as to flatten it. She holds up the torn-out section of the paper so the audience can see a large photograph of a young woman, good looking in a plain fashion, wearing a hard smile of triumph, then she reads aloud in a hoarse, stricken voice.*] Mr. and Mrs. James Finley announce the engagement of their daughter, Miss Constance Finley, to Mr.—T. Ralph Ellis, principal of—

[*Pause. There is much stage business. Dorothea is stunned for some moments but then comes to violent life and action. She picks up the picnic shoebox, thrusts it fiercely into Bodey's hands, opens the door for her but rushes back to pick up Bodey's small black straw hat trimmed with paper daises, then opens the door for Bodey again with a violent gesture meaning, "Go quick!" Bodey goes. In the hall we hear various articles falling from Bodey's hold and a small, panting gasp. Then there is silence. Helena gets up with a mechanical air of sympathy.*]

HELENA: That woman is sly all right but not as sly as she's stupid. She might have guessed you'd want the society page and notice Mr. Ellis's engagement had been torn out. Anyhow, the news would have reached you at the school tomorrow. Of course I can't understand how you could be taken in by what-ever little attentions you may have received from Ralph Ellis.

DOROTHEA: —"Little—attentions?" I assure you they were not—"little attentions," they were—

HELENA: Little attentions which you magnified in your imagi-nation. Well, now, let us dismiss the matter, which has dismissed itself! Dorothea, about the postdated check, I'm not sure the real estate agents would be satisfied with that. Now surely, Dorothea, surely you have relatives who could help you with a down payment in cash?

DOROTHEA: —Helena, I'm not interested in Westmoreland Place. —Now.

HELENA: What!

DOROTHEA: I've—abandoned that idea. I've decided not to move.

HELENA [*aghast*]: —Do you realize what a shockingly irresponsible thing you are doing? Don't you realize that you are placing me in a very unfair position? You led me to believe I could count on your sharing the expense of the place, and now, at the last moment, when I have no time to get hold of someone else, you suddenly—pull out. It's really irresponsible of you. It's a really very irresponsible thing to do.

DOROTHEA: —I'm afraid we wouldn't have really gotten along together. I'm not uncomfortable here. It's only two blocks from the school and—I won't be needing a place I can't afford to entertain—anyone now. —I think I would like to be alone.

HELENA: All I can say is, the only thing I can say is—

DOROTHEA: Don't say it, just, just—leave me alone, now, Helena.

HELENA: Well, that I shall do. You may be right, we wouldn't have gotten along. Perhaps Miss Bodenheifer and her twin brother are much more on your social and cultural level than I'd hoped. And of course there's always the charm of Miss Gluck from upstairs.

DOROTHEA: The prospect of that is not as dismaying to me, Helena, as the little card parties and teas you'd had in mind for us on Westmoreland Place . . .

HELENA: *Chacun à son goût.*

DOROTHEA: Yes, yes.

HELENA [*at the door*]: There is rarely a graceful way to say good-bye. [*She exits.*]

[*Pause. Dorothea shuts her eyes very tight and raises a clenched hand in the air, nodding her head several times as if affirming an unhappy suspicion regarding the way of the world. This gesture suffices to discharge her sense of defeat. Now she springs up determinedly and goes to the phone.*

[*While waiting for a connection, she notices Miss Gluck seated disconsolately in a corner of the kitchenette.*]

DOROTHEA: Now Miss Gluck, now Sophie, we must pull ourselves together and go on. Go on, we must just go on, that's all that life seems to offer and—demand. [*She turns her attention to the phone.*] Hello, operator, can you get me information, please? —Hello? Information? Can you get me the number of the little station at the end of the Delmar car-line where you catch the, the—open streetcar that goes out to Creve Coeur Lake? —Thank you.

MISS GLUCK [*speaking English wih difficulty and a heavy German accent*]: Please don't leave me alone. I can't go up!

DOROTHEA [*her attention still occupied with the phone*]: Creve Coeur car-line station? Look. On the platform in a few minutes will be a plumpish little woman with a big artificial flower over one ear and a stoutish man with her, probably with a cigar. I have to get an important message to them. Tell them that Dotty called and has decided to go to Creve Coeur with them after all so will they please wait. You'll have to shout to the woman because she's—*deaf* . . .

[*For some reason the word "deaf" chokes her and she begins to sob as she hangs up the phone. Miss Gluck rises, sobbing louder.*]

No, no, Sophie, come here. [*Impulsively she draws Miss Gluck into her arms.*] I know, Sophie, I know, crying is a release, but it—inflames the eyes.

[*She takes Miss Gluck to the armchair and seats her there. Then she goes to the kitchenette, gets a cup of coffee and a cruller, and brings them to Sophie.*]

Make yourself comfortable, Sophie.

[*She goes to the bedroom, gets a pair of gloves, then returns and crosses to the kitchen table to collect her hat and pocketbook. She goes to the door, opens it, and says . . .*]

We'll be back before dark.

THE LIGHTS DIM OUT

New Directions Paperbooks — A Partial Listing

For complete listing request free catalog from
New Directions, 80 Eighth Avenue, New York 10011

†Bilingual

For complete listing request free catalog from
New Directions, 80 Eighth Avenue, New York 10011

†Biling